SOFTLY GLOWING
EXIT SIGNS

Praise for Softly Glowing Exit Signs

"The takeaway from reading *Softly Glowing Exit Signs*, is that the writing is real life, and that overall poetry is real life, and that real life can be measured and unmasked within writing itself. When reading *Softly Glowing Exit Signs* I felt I was left in a room with Georgia Park, and she is telling me everything with a vulnerability she has not shown many people. It left me needing to read more, or sit and listen because anything else would be unjust.

Conclusively, *Softly Glowing Exit Signs* feels exactly like spending hours, being up all night, with a person bearing their soul, to which all you can be is silent, and listen, and all you can say is, "Thanks for sharing all of this with me."

—Timothy Gager

"You will quickly find when you get to the end of the first prose piece in this book, that Park is serving the imagery of her work without warning labels or protective coatings. Raw and visceral are the best words to describe how she delivers her amazing talent in "Softly Glowing Exit Signs" and it packs a very powerful punch early out of the gate.
She takes the reader on a journey of heightened emotions and unflinching looks into the everyday reality of our world. The settings and the props for the stage of this performance would seem to be

mundane facets of daily life. But, with Park's expert hand, they are arranged to form vast murals of expression that one would not normally consider when taking in such sights.

In short, "Softly Glowing Exit Signs" is a masterpiece work by Georgia Park and should be included in the library of all of those who admire the intricacies of human existence and the beautiful moments that can be found in even the most challenging of circumstances."

—Eric Syrdal, author of *Pantheon*

SOFTLY GLOWING EXIT SIGNS

Georgia Park

Havertown, Pennsylvania

© 2020 Softly Glowing Exit Signs by Georgia Park

Editors: Christine E. Ray
Kindra M. Austin
Cover design: Mitch Green

All rights reserved.

No part of this book may be used, stored in a system retrieval system, or transmitted, in any form or in any means—by electronic, mechanical, photocopying, recording, or reproduced in any manner whatsoever—without written permission from the author, except in the case of brief quotations embodied in critical articles and reviews.

For information, address Indie Blu(e) Publishing.
indieblucollective@gmail.com

Published in the United States of America by Indie Blu(e) Publishing.

ISBN: 978-1-951724-02-3
Library of Congress Control Number: 2020933375

For all of you who showed me generosity and
kindness after my house fire,
with special thanks to:

*Candice Daquin, Christine E. Ray, Kindra M.
Austin, Nicole Lyons, Joey Gould, Penny
McCarthy, JD Scrimgeour, Kevin Carey, Julie
Matuschak, Marc Levy, Kevin McCarthy, Cat
Dossett, MP Carver, Jasper Kerkau, Nadia
Garofalo, Erin McManus, Melissa Carella, Nikki,
Rob, and Karen O'Keefe, Paul Mahoney, Marilyn
Rea Beyer, Lisa May, Megha Sood, Ethan Feldbau,
Joseph O'Day, Stephanie Angelini, Roopsi Risam,
Tim Gager, Erik Stelling, Liz-Mary Jelinek,
Michael Mclellan, & The Hawthorne Hotel of
Salem, Massachusetts*

TABLE OF CONTENTS

GREASE FIRE	13
MORNING COUGH	14
HER MINK PAW COAT	15
FROM THE OUTFIELD	18
(UN)EASE	19
THAT'S NOT POETRY!	20
SYLVIA IS OUR CAR	22
DEAD FISH	24
BURNING ORANGE	25
MICROSCOPIC CHANGES	26
WEDDING PLANS	27
LATE	28
THE LAST REUNION	30

- **QUICK, THINK OF SOMETHING** — 32
- **DON'T MIND HER** — 34
- **DOWN IN COSTA RICA** — 51
- **FOR HOW STUPID I WAS, & LOST** — 53
- **IF YOU SMOKE** — 55
- **YOUR FAVORITE MEMORY** — 60
- **THE BARBEQUE** — 64
- **THE BUDDHA'S LAP** — 66
- **SKYLINE AGAIN** — 69
- **ARE YOU GONNA EAT THAT?** — 71
- **I JUST GOT BACK** — 72
- **DANGEROUS ADVENTURES** — 74
- **WALK OF SHAME** — 77
- **EVERYBODY TALKS** — 78
- **IT'S JUST ANOTHER FUN SUMMER** — 79

ANOTHER PSYCHIATRIST	80
OUR GHOST CHILDREN	81
THE PROS AND CONS OF BEING THIS HEAVILY MEDICATED	83
FRIENDLY ADVICE	85
DOING WITHOUT	88
DAFFODIL	90
DÉCOR AND DECORUM	123
THE CASHIER AND THE WOMAN	125
WHEN THE FIRE DISPLACED US	126
LOST AND FOUND IN THE RUBBLE	127
THE SMELL OF DISASTER	129
HOW TO KEEP WORKING THROUGH A CRISIS	130
SPIRALING QUESTIONS	131
COMMUNITY	133

FIRE AND REBIRTH   134

TURNING TRICKS   136

PUT THE NEWSPAPER DOWN FIRST   137

BITS OF BUTTERFLY   138

MORNINGS   139

VACATION OVER   140

THIS HOUSE   141

FRACTIONS   142

THE SIXTIES   143

PUPPY SUPPLIES   145

DESK JOB   146

A LACK OF ETIQUETTE   147

THIS WON'T BE THE EVENT OF THE YEAR   148

ON BECOMING A WIFE   150

MAKE MORE MONEY   151

THE DAY'S ENDING	152
THE CROW'S FUNERAL	154
HANGING ON	155
THE END OF AN ERA	156
THAT'S ALL, FOLKS!	158
WHERE TO?	159

FIRE!

Grease Fire

My mother is not at the sink
not with eyes sunken
or a frilly apron

it's my brother at the stovetop
aged eight, frying fish
while I am upstairs
with the door closed

I am counting
all I do is practice
I can't zipper zips
or button buttons
for the test I have coming up
to get into kindergarten

I am worrying when the grease fire
explodes
I can just hear my brother calling
get out of the house!
as he runs through the back door
but I can't make out his words
so I ignore them
the smoke makes its way to my room
I don't notice until the firemen come

and I don't notice
that all the other kids can read
until the teacher
separates me from them
and asks if I'm even trying

Morning Cough

Last Christmas I woke up coughing
And my foster sister asked if I was sick
"No," I said, "sometimes, that happens."
I don't say it's from a lifetime of smoking
"Oh, ok. That's just your morning cough.
Ready for breakfast?"
Those were my father's words
Coming out of her mouth
Oh, it's just a morning cough
Means there's nothing to worry about

Her Mink Paw Coat

How long will her mink paw coat
hold her talcum powder
and glamour scent from eight years ago

it is unflattering on me
much too big to hug my frame
and provide the warmth
that made the coat
worth what she spent on it

but I removed the cellophane
and took it out of my closet
in honor of Veteran's Day
because she was so patriotic
my grandmother was a veteran
I like to tell people who don't believe it
and no one I know thinks the amount of money
spent on
the tiny mink lives lost (how many? a hundred?)
could be worth it

so I tell them it's not genuine
all the while I stroke the fine hairs covering
my breast, my hips, discovering the touch of a skin
much softer than the one I was born with
the scent of her as the woman
who fought so rabidly to instill me

with her fiery passion for conquering
not only my wilderness, but also, the minks'

Ghost Town

I don't have a childhood bedroom to show you
my elementary school was blasted
my best friend and I saw it happen
one scorching summer day
so hot we took off our shirts and pants
and watched the tow trucks
cart the rubble out toward the highway
we'd intended to go swimming
but we couldn't turn away

my little brother went to elementary school
in the new building
but he's grown up now
I don't know where he's gone
but I have a car and I know this spot
behind that building where the weeds grow wild
and there might not be a trail anymore
but there was one once
that led to a cornfield and then by dusk
we could get to the Appalachian trail
and we could just keep walking
to where we could watch the sun
rise and set again onto the factory
which is now defunct

Georgia Park

From the Outfield

I want to bench press you
above my head
I want to slam you
into a book I don't understand
pressing, topped by
dictionaries and vases
until you become paper thin
I want to hang onto something
I shouldn't
I want to dry the stems and leaves
extending from your body
prickly
I want to detract from the richness of hues
in your head
bowing
so I can keep you on my mantel
in a glass jar
as a memento
conquered
of an afternoon game spent
in the outfield
picking wild flowers
while my parents screamed
"Keep your eye on the ball!
It's coming!"

(Un)ease

That girl is giggling, it sets me at (un)ease—who said never trust a little girl crying in the corner? it was my brother

—it was the fire licking up the side of the building it was the smoke inhalation she was gagging she was already done, he should have left her—

who said she was giggling?
who said I wasn't at ease?

who said there's a woman almost thirty selling trinkets and suitcases on the internet thinking about cicadas just the sound of them and not even wishing she could leave?
thinking of running on the pavement of that hot, hellish city (stop it! breathe...)

That's Not Poetry!

"That's not poetry!" she sneered at the woman
who got up on stage to read a found piece
her father's last grocery list before he died
"Chocolate-for Maggie, pecans,
spaghetti, something to hang the painting with-"
"That's not a list poem, it's just a list!"
she heckled from the audience

"Well, it's a good effort, I suppose." She chuckled
at the student who had written fifty-seven pages of prose
in front of all the other students who had just finished
telling him to keep writing, that this seemed important
and after the student agreed, "Yeah it is. Writing this
has really helped me make peace with my past."

"That's not art, it's a blue splotch!" She guffawed
pretending to be scandalized at the price of admission
at that avant-garde museum in the Berkshires
secretly thrilled she would be able to reference it for years
get a good laugh, and drop the name of her timeshare

Softly Glowing Exit Signs

"Good job, professor," we all told her
after we were forced to attend her poetry reading
even if her poems were flat, did not use the five senses
imagery, personification, or any of the things
she'd been teaching us—least of all, emotion

Sylvia is OUR Car

Your anger is our gray, outdated Volvo
held together by rope
duct tape and you
yelling at it
it's laughable
this car
once a sign of status!?

your words no longer melt me
it all seems now so petty
embarrassing, the doors
stop working
at inconvenient times
I finally let go of your pride
and try to exit through the window
when my foot
gets stuck in my mouth again
the car starts moving

Vroooom!!

you are stuck in reverse and desperate
people are watching
I struggle back onto the rank upholstery
I'm red in the face
demanding
"Just take me home now

Softly Glowing Exit Signs

I'm ready"
another night ending
prematurely
over nothing
they say
it's not worth fixing
but to the shop we go
this time seat belted, ready
my heart, a stone

this lemon's most expensive
let's scrap it, darling
then you can afford that hearse
I know you wanted to buy me

Dead Fish

I felt like a fish
you had scooped out
of our aquarium
and pinned down lazily
with your pinkie finger

while you talked to other women
I was just trying to get to a place
where I could breathe again

all of our fish
died soon enough anyway
from your loud music
and my screaming
I cried all night for them
while you stayed out
moshing to punk rock

Burning Orange

The NPR specialist
says shame outweighs
both love and anger

I let it glow orange
lick and curl
the edges of my manuscript
and run into the arms of my ex-boyfriend

who doesn't know my verses
and never speaks of
the person I showed them to
that I shouldn't have

Microscopic Changes

I didn't just shatter a glass
I stepped on it so now there is
a microscopic shard of glass
that stings whenever I take a step
but I can't find it
I also blistered my fingers on the baking pan
and smoked so much I couldn't breathe
my hands have lost their stability
my voice has gained a sandpapery quality
except in private, it found this terrible vulnerability
high pitched and soft, like a kitten mewing
and I am no longer good or clean

Wedding Plans

He asks, "How much are you against being married by a Catholic priest?"
        She studies him for a moment.
              "Very."

Late
For Nadia

I'm late for my finals
late for the third train
this year to Chicago
I still have glitter
mixed in with my oatmeal
from a misspent night
in New York City
and skulls and crossbones
chattering my teeth
from a stop in Salem
where at least a girl
smiled at me
I'm late for my period
late on realizing
a fair few things
I needed to realize
before I went
through with them
I was absent for
my own wedding
I didn't even leave
a note or anything
I recently lost
my driver's license
only one of my eyes
is currently working

Softly Glowing Exit Signs

I don't know the difference
between my real self
and my pseudonym
I can't speak
any languages
so I just end up
nodding
until I fall asleep
in front of everyone
at all the most
important meetings
but when she meets me
at the train station
she just says
it's good
so good
to see you
again

The Last Reunion

I was always egg shaped
hunched over a book
with my knees drawn to my chest
I never left an impression
on my own small section of this country
not more than the hoofs onto the pasture
on a hot, dry day
left by the animals of my neighbors
who I could never identify
let alone name

but she left an impression
like ten bulls when the field was muddy
our local newspaper even wrote
an article on her and all the local diners
hung it in glass or laminate
and I went as her date
onto my own street
towards the swings
away from my family

I told her, let's not stay out too late
and then, when she got caught up
with all of our high school bullies
who have apologized to her since
but never me, I got drunk
and I hooked up with two of them

Softly Glowing Exit Signs

consecutively in the back
of their pickup trucks

and when she found me
it was just like then
she kissed me good night
and tucked me into my side
of her bed

Quick, Think of Something

It's a cheerful sunset
through the luxurious floor-to-ceiling windows
of my temporary office
featuring golden bursts of blue
the same hues of a parakeet
I once attached sentimentality to

I hold myself, watching
and remember that once
I loved well and was cherished

I hold myself knowing
I can't get that back again
I grant, maybe that's enough
for one lifetime—maybe it's time
to wish for something different

I cajole myself into daydreaming
while the light still warms my cheek
ok, so what's the next great thing?

*

Someday, I think
I'd like to leave
this little carnival city
I'd miss my friends

Softly Glowing Exit Signs

but I think that, someday
I should do it
or maybe, maybe...
she'll come back to me
then, of course
everything would be different--
I'd want different things
or maybe, maybe...

the sun sets
I leave the office
I come back again
repeat the sunset

Don't Mind Her

I try to get up as early as possible to avoid the people on the train. I tend to brown out in a crowd; not a blackout exactly, but an emotional brownout. That's what my therapist calls it. By the time I get to where I'm going, I'd be hard pressed to say how exactly I got there. It doesn't hurt that most of my focus settles on how fast my heart is beating, how uncomfortable I am, the heat rash I tend to get between my legs, the ass sweat. The embarrassing way the train moves my body around while my skeleton stands stock still. But all in all, it's easier for me to process people as blurs of colors, passing, so I don't have to focus on them.

I see a bit of flannel here, a high heeled shoe, cornrows, a hand. If I look too closely, I know I'll see details that will upset me. The wedding ring on the hand, the pretty little girl inside of the yellow rain jacket. Too pretty. Not that it matters, I remind myself. Their vulnerability lies in the fact that they're little, not pretty. I hate seeing little girls the most.

I am no longer pretty, if I ever was. All my life, I never really saw myself in the mirror, just shapes. Even so, I'm sure that pretty would attract too much attention, that I wouldn't like it. I wonder again if pretty even matters.

I think being a woman, being useable, being little, is the problem.

I am no longer little.

My folds of flesh double up on themselves, I have to lift my breasts to wash underneath, and then every roll of my stomach. I rarely bother anymore. All this extra skin, all these folds, they have a mind of their own. They keep their own secrets. Sometimes I'll find things in there. A coin, a kernel of popcorn. Nothing good. I never find, say, a winning lottery ticket or a heartfelt apology from my father. So, I don't wash much. I probably smell. The thought doesn't bother me.

This morning I have failed in one more way than my usual. I haven't woken up early enough to avoid the masses. The pretty landscapes will be lost on me. They'll be washed away with my clear vision by the rain of people. I start to see them at the station.

A brown coat. Running sneakers. A purse shaped like a watermelon, with a gold chain. A bald spot. I sit on a bench and look at my hands. No wedding ring there.

I see a little child. A toddler. I look away. What does my therapist say? Breathe in, count to four, hold for two, breathe out, counting to four. Close my eyes? What am I trying to achieve here? Is it a spell to make the child disappear? Is it a girl or a boy? It doesn't matter. Is she pretty?

Inhale...two, three....hold. Exhale...
No one bothers me. Not literally. No one reaches out to touch me, talk about the weather. They haven't in years. I'm glad of it. Idle chit chat is more bothersome to me than anything. More often than not, I'd rather be reading. Adventure books, oddly. Children's books for boys. Pirates and mermaids, hidden treasures, excellent journeys, that kind of thing.

To look at me, you might think I was secretly an avid Twilight reader. I imagine I come off as extremely lonely and not too bright. In truth, I haven't thought about sex for years. Not really.

The train comes. I can't tell you how the ride was. I browned out. Next thing I knew, I'd arrived.

Over Eaters Anonymous.

A shitty, single piece of printer paper taped to the glass of an office door, in the basement of a shopping plaza. Again, couldn't tell you how I got down the steps, but I notice there are no special fonts on the sign, no decorations.

I can also tell you that I turn the doorknob. I grab it, hold it in my fist, and turn it. This is what my therapist refers to as grounding, mindfulness. Just paying attention to what you're doing. "Why bother?" I'd asked her. "So, when you lose your keys and people ask you where you've been, you can tell them. It can help you keep track of things." "I don't talk to people." I told her, "it wouldn't help."

And this is where she changed the subject. "Have you been going to Overeaters Anonymous?" she'd asked.

So, here I am. And here is Donna, I can tell by the hippy skirt, swishing to reveal a peek of hairy legs followed by sandals with socks. Our group leader.

And then, of course, there are some other people. Donna is already talking over them by the time I come in.

"Hello everyone! Good to see you back. Have a seat, now, and we can start with the serenity prayer."

The feet shuffle, people murmur, good to see you, how have you been, all that bullshit. Even though they'll find out more than they ever wanted to know about how everyone has been in just a few short seconds. What is the point of these pleasantries? I'm only interested in their confessions.

"Ok, who wants to give us the serenity prayer today?" And before Gwen can volunteer, Donna is saying my name. I'm not surprised. Gwen talks the most and I talk the least. Donna is a good leader and understands this dynamic.

I'm secretly thankful to be called on, but not willing to let on that I appreciate the effort, the chance to take my turn and be heard. I say the prayer quietly, quickly, "'God grant us the serenity to accept the things we cannot change, the courage to change the things we can, and the wisdom to know the difference.'"

"Ok, and Gwen," I guess Donna either feels some tension or feels Gwen has waited as long as was healthy for her to wait, "Would you like to read us the steps?"

Softly Glowing Exit Signs

"Sure, I will," says Gwen, clearing her throat. I sullenly tune it out. I hate Gwen. I hate the pastel tee shirts she tucks into the elastic band of her flower printed pants. I hate that her outfits suggest gardening while her white gooseflesh insists that this woman has never seen the sun. And she's such a martyr. If I believe, and sometimes I do, that she is suffering more than she enjoys suffering, I would be able to enjoy her long monologues more. My therapist says I hate that she talks more than I do, hogs the attention where I won't. Sometimes, I hate my therapist, too.

The steps are another long monologue I've lost patience with. The gist of it is that we are all pieces of shit who like pieces of chicken, though we're not allowed to describe in detail what kind. Mention a leg or a juicy, fried breast, and it's "trigger talk." You get three warnings for using trigger talk before you're expelled. I'm on my second. I've decided that if I can't describe food in great detail, if I can't express what's really on my mind, the greasy burger patties layered on top of each other, divided by cheese, the butterscotch sundaes, the supersized order followed by three apple pies, or no, apple pies first because they're so hot they burn on the way down...well, there's nothing else worth saying. But I could listen.

I could listen to Gwen talk about how her family is falling apart. I generally like that, for the first ten minutes. I like to hear about the daughter with anorexia and how she had said it was her mother's fault. The names she calls her, sticking like so many meatballs in Gwen's throat. Pig, disgusting, an embarrassment. I realize that these words apply to me, as well, but since I live alone, it's really not an issue. I like to hear about the son's drug problem. Then I usually get bored or feel like Gwen is enjoying the attention too much for me to bask in her misery.

"Ok," says Donna, "So we've all admitted we are powerless against food and it's an addiction, right? And most of us," here, I appreciate the lack of an accusatory pause or tone of voice. But there is a fumble. A falsely hopeful tone, which, in a way, is worse. "Most of us are trying to replace our addiction with a trust in God. But our struggles with food addiction have occupied most of our minds, and now you all might feel like there's a big gaping hole there. What should we think about instead? Has anyone picked up any hobbies?"

Wendall raises an arm from his sweaty grey tee shirt. I never look directly at him, but I have a feeling he licks his lips a lot. "If I may...excuse me, but this might be a little embarrassing." He laughs melodiously. Here it comes, I think. He's another knitter. Why can't he steal office supplies like that woman who stopped coming? I liked her. Do you like her because you know she quit? My inner therapist asks. No. Well, that too. I liked her because she was interesting. An admitted thief.

I find Wendall's confession far less appealing. "I think about sex, a lot. I know this might not be appropriate, but you know, it's been my saving grace. It fills that hole. I spend a lot of time on chatlines. I've discovered I have something of a fetish..." Here is where I look at my lap, carefully avoiding Wendell's arm, right to my left. I zone in. I'm wearing sweatpants of the grey variety. Cuddly on the inside. Too hot sometimes. Well, what else am I supposed to wear?

Hey Wendall? I want to say, Shut up. Don't ruin this for me. It's my one thing.

I gather, from Donna's tone, that she's basically telling Wendall to shut up too. In a laughing, light, yet warning tone. I like Donna. I can't say I know exactly what she said to diffuse the situation, but I know she was right, and Wendall was wrong, and now everything is going to go back to normal. Maybe Craig will talk about his comic books.

Then, there it is again, my name. By the tone of it, Donna's probably said it twice already.

"Yes." I'm listening. I look at her white cheek to show that I'm at attention.

"Have you found a way to replace food? Or want to share with us a confession? Nothing too graphic, of course."

So many choices. "I'll go for the confession, I guess." I put my hands on my lap and look at them. No rings at all. Chubby, gross. I put my hands away and look at my soft sweatpants again. "Sometimes, when I order pizza, I pretend someone else is there. Just so that the delivery boy doesn't know all that food is for me. Two large pizzas, three subs, two of them roast beef, one with swiss, one-"

"Ok! Remember not to get into too much detail. It sounds like you really need a hobby to take your mind off food. Tell me, is there anything else you enjoy doing?"

I don't tell them that I like to read adventure books because in my life, making it to Overeaters Anonymous each week is my biggest adventure. I don't tell them that I haven't even seen my vagina in years. And I definitely don't tell them about my fantasy. To visit my father in the nursing home.

"Donna? I think I'm done sharing for today. Thank you." I smile. My therapist had suggested this tactic. I have a feeling Donna smiles back. I don't think about anything for the rest of the meeting. I am not grounded. I float.

The meeting adjourns. I know, because I hear the fold up chairs groaning, moving a quarter of an inch backwards as their former occupants lift their bodies off the things.

I try to get out while people are still hovering, socializing. More pleasantries, how is your wife? So, do anything fun over the weekend? Plans for fourth of July? I turn away from them to make my exit, unnoticed, as I always manage to do. If someone stops me, I usually make some euphemism about nature calling and let my face explicitly suggest the need to express explosive diarrhea. Immediately and abundantly. That generally works. I don't know why I didn't think of that this time.

I always remember to ground on the doorknob. I like grasping the cool metal, the act of turning it, the feeling of unlatching a secret bond, releasing.

The freedom, afterwards, on the way out. I look forward to it.

But a beefy, black hand beats mine to the punch. It's Wendall, being what I'm sure he would call a gentleman.

"Thank you." I mutter. I'm still thinking about his sex speech, his fetish. I guess he caught me off guard.

"Sure thing. I was just heading out, too, let me walk you to your car?"

"I took the train."

"Oh? Where are you coming from?" And this is how it starts. The pleasantries. Everyone at this group is trying to bond, form a community, make you think you matter. Because everyone at this group has been excluded and felt like they haven't. The meaningless words somehow make them feel better. Important, loved, even. I don't know. It just annoys me. I don't say anything.

"Are you feeling shy today? That's ok, I know you tend to be on the quiet side. Sometimes, I feel shy too. But you know, a little human contact might be just what you need. I know I did. It's made a world of difference. If you'd just open up, I could be your friend." Wendall's voice softens on that last word, 'friend.'

In fact, something's off about his whole delivery. He's speaking softly, persuasively. Is he hitting on me? Of all the crazy things? Well, I guess the horny fat guy thinks he might as well shoot for the quietest fat woman, isolate her, build up her self-esteem? Like taking candy from a baby, he must think.

How does he know, if I even wanted sex, which I don't....if I've even thought about sex, which I haven't...that I wouldn't prefer a nice, thin man, whose ribs I could stroke while we're fucking? Someone half the size of me? Someone I could control? Or a woman. I've been disinterested for so long, I wouldn't even know in which direction to go with it.

Who's to say that even if I was interested, I'd have to be paired off with the first person who comes along and shows interest in me? I'm not even interested, anyways. But if I was.

"Come on, tell me. What do you do for fun? You have to do something. You know, if you want to replace the food addiction, that's the next step."

I turn around and look him in the eye. Brown eyes, almost purplish, maroon. The shape of a nose. A hairline. "You know what I like to do?" My voice is louder, quicker than I've ever heard it. I can't predict what I'm about to say. I hadn't planned on even speaking to this man. But the words come, "I like to go to Petco. I like to go to the hamster cages, you know, in the corner? Where no one really can see you, behind the cages. I like to find the cutest one. Maybe brown spots, maybe young, maybe cuddly. I like to sneak my hand in and pick that one up. Then, I like to squeeze the life out of it. Of course, you have to stick a finger in the mouth, so it doesn't squeak too loud. But I like to hear a little. I like to watch her eyes go still. Then, I put her body back in the cage, with the other hamsters. I buy some cat food. I go home. But I don't have a cat. I don't care for animals. Except the cute little hamsters. I like them. A lot."

Wendall doesn't say anything. It doesn't matter if he does. I've already turned on my heel and walked as quickly as I've walked in years towards the train station. I don't want to be followed. I know that I won't. This isn't the movies. I don't want Wendall to follow me. That's why I put him off. I have no idea where the hamster stuff came from. Good job, though, I told myself. Good story.

Softly Glowing Exit Signs

There are other Overeaters Anonymous groups I can go to. There will be other Donnas. I'll find a group, maybe, of just women. No disgusting sex addicts like Wendall. He'd have to be pretty sick, pretty desperate just to approach me. I'd gotten away with years of not being approached. I find the thought of him even thinking about me that way quite disturbing.

I go to my happy place, to make the train ride bearable. To ignore everything. To relax.
In my happy place, I imagine visiting my father in the nursing home. He is old, he is comatose. He is thin and frail. I don't talk to the nurses. I'm not the cheery daughter with the floral print pants like lonely Gwen, talking her head off, chattering like a starling.

No, I go in quietly, and I sit by his bed. I hold his hand. I've grown out my nails, I don't care if dirt collects underneath them. Because when I hold his hand, I want to dig my claws into the fleshy, underside of it. I want to see his brow furrow with the pain of it. I want to sit there like that. I want it to leave marks. I want the dirt of my fingernails to go into his blood.

EVERYBODY

Softly Glowing Exit Signs

Down in Costa Rica

People wanted to know about Costa Rica
but I didn't tell them about the parrots
the clown school right up the street
from our hostel, the teens
who would stop traffic just to juggle
or the park where my lover gazed at a couple
making out heavily on the bench and said
"I can't remember the last time
I enjoyed kissing someone like that."

I didn't tell them how he almost got us
kicked off the flight from Florida
how he threatened to flush my credit card
down the toilet and asked how long
I thought I could survive without him
how we were banned from our hostel
for fighting that night, I locked the door
to our cabin and he snaked up the tree outside
to try to crawl through the window
of our bathroom while I stood screaming
at him to stay out

neither did I tell them
about the coke dealer, his moustache
long pinkie nails and golden rings
the cigars he claimed to be selling
or how we had a white Christmas

with him as our skinny Santa
and the lines all split up
on our engraved bedside table

no, I sent them song lyrics
and asked them what they thought
David Bowie meant when he said
that man sold the world
and told them our pictures
couldn't be uploaded
and that I probably wasn't
going to get the chance
to write again

Softly Glowing Exit Signs

For How Stupid I Was, & Lost

I drink because I can't write poetry of places like he does
I can't even read his poetry without flinching
even though I crouched in an alley in some city in Spain
looking at the moon and drinking, inciting rage
and loss and hunger and the mourning that comes with
all these things and because I was so young
I was influenced by Jack Kerouac on top of it

I drink because my recitations have escaped me
and oh, how I used to love poetry and being hidden
and not seeing anything--and the strange places and
the fragmentation and how insane I had gone
when I let him fuck me in a cornfield on the farm
and my finger was ringless and I stopped staring at it
and started looking up and the sky wasn't
any different, not even at all

I drink because everyone who's here now
wouldn't have been at my most lost
I drink because so many times, during sex
I realized I didn't want to be doing it
while I still was

which left me impotent
when the real thing came along

I drink because of how far I've traveled
and because I am no longer young
all blank-headed and stupid and alone
I drink because I'm sick of being responsible

and because when he closed the shutters on the cafe
and locked it up, and played his songs
I have never danced with a man like that since
and we never even made love

Softly Glowing Exit Signs

If You Smoke

The nurses and doctors looked like ants
all slim with exactingly clean uniforms
long, silken black hair on each nurse
doctors with their bobs and crew cuts
in the blindingly white, sterile-smelling hive
of the emergency room

where the bees seemed to be the patients
bellies swollen, overtaken, still in their mismatching
pajama tops and bottoms, one shoe on, one off
cups of tea brewing for the friends and family
who had escorted them and then were left
in the outlier, waiting, sipping on honeyed tea

my boss took me in by the crook of my arm
clucking her tongue—hard-workers don't get sick
there was mold in the apartment she provided me
but I also routinely drank soju, wet my hair
and hung out of the 43rd story window smoking

the people I used to watch who looked like ants
from so far up
took their tiny cars in and out of the subway stations
and onto the highways, and entered lit up clubs and
strip joints

I could see everything but the hospital my boss took me to
the nurses didn't take me from her until several needles
were plunged into my arm and I was even more sedated
than I already was--I heard *megook, wagukin salam, waygooken*
or Foreigner, American, America swirling around in a buzz of Korean

I could only imagine their conversation:
why are there so many foreigners lately?
this is the third American I've seen this week.
Oh, because America is turning into such a dangerous country
even with Obama, even this morning, there was a terrible shooting.
Americans are going crazy, maybe she's a refugee?
No, it's because we are thriving as a country. She came here for the opportunities
maybe, and for the shows and the music. What's wrong with her, then?
Pneumonia in both lungs, and she smells like she's been drinking.

a doctor who spoke some English carted me off to the x-ray machines

Softly Glowing Exit Signs

and with great pride and flourish asked me to take
off my breasts
I sighed exhausted and said I couldn't. From then
on he used a translator
which, after my x-ray was taken, said in its
mechanical voice
"if you smoke, you will die"
I was fitted by a silent nurse into a hospital gown
and led into a glass box with tubes, a chinstrap
and a cylinder where my mouth should've gone
the nurse painstakingly mimed that I should blow
into the cylinder
I tried, and it hurt like fire. she mimed to blow
harder
I started crying and pretended to pass out
after much commotion I was moved to a bed

my needles were replaced. colors splashed
with each action that was performed on my body
maroon when they dragged me, peach sinking into
the sheeted bed, purple when they plunged the
needles in
porcelain colored, and then ash gray

I had been failing days before they found me
I stopped using the bathroom. I liked to wear my
engagement ring
and hold my hand with a limp wrist towards the
space heater

on my bedside table until I could feel the white gold heat
I wanted to see if it would melt--I pulled it out when I thought
that I was dying. I wanted to be buried with the reason
I wound up so far away in such a strange situation

stranger than dying in that single bed
was potentially dying in this
the cleanest hospital I'd ever been in
where no visitors come to see me
although my boss insisted over her irate phone calls
that she needed me back in working condition
I removed my needles, snuck onto the city streets
in my hospital gown and I smoked very often
you would think somebody would've cottoned on
and tried to stop me. there were no more commotions
after my admittance. the nurses swarmed around
to replace my needles. my boss kept calling
because I was such a costly investment
I saw the shade of rusted metal and coagulated blood
for every forced pill, every therapy, every revival
until finally, one day I failed to succumb
and just like that I was kicked out of the hospital

and told to go home "hah!" I muttered, "with what passport?"
then my boss was ushering me into a car
apologizing to the nurses
that afternoon I taught the alphabet to twenty-seven kindergartners

Your Favorite Memory

You peer into the indoor pond
while your boyfriend is in the bathroom
it's a wonder you don't fall in
you've both been drinking
but you see at least seven of them
koi fish, each as wide as both your arms linked
and more muscular than you'll ever be
the owner of the bar doesn't have the language
to tell you he either thinks you're pretty
or very young but you can see it
in how he scrambles to hand you the pellets
to feed the fish
you let him think, in your girlish delight
that he was right--you are either pretty
or very young, a child, really
and the fish converge towards the pellets
falling from your small, balled up fist
you remember reading somewhere
that doctors prescribe feeding koi fish
to wealthy people with the means to build the ponds
and stress related heart conditions
by the time your boyfriend comes back from the bathroom
you don't care that the two of you had been fighting
for three days running
you're completely relaxed and he thinks

Softly Glowing Exit Signs

you and the koi fish are both so stunning
that he is finally, finally quiet
so you hand him some pellets
and then the swift movement
these glittering, golden muscles of fish
are swimming toward his own balled up fist
and he flattens it to release the pellets
then he takes your hand with his

The Chinese Smog

The Chinese smog swirled in
long before I immigrated
with the blue Korean skies
to form the gray white dome
that locked me into that country
the picture in my passport captured
me cowering and turning my face away
from American politics
to gaze into the waves
of the ocean that could topple me
and being shaken, instead
by the North Korean bomb tests
I tell my therapist
"I was safe there, I was happy"
and she says, "that isn't true
though, not really
you're just romanticizing
because you feel lost"
my memories shift
and swirl continuously
casting a new light
on each country

I hear cicadas in my ears
from my Puerto Rican engagement
I tilt my head
and hear the prostitutes calling
from a haze of red lights in Thailand
and walk past them into a cloud forest
on the Nicaraguan mountains

Softly Glowing Exit Signs

I look up and I'm domed in
these American skies
are as white today
as that old pollution
I look down
and I see my knees
shaking

The Barbeque

Silke was a 6 foot tall German woman
with a 5'3 Brazilian lover
they were my favorite couple
because of the height difference
their tender exchange of languages
and the way she spoke very boldly
while he barbecued meat for her friends
which, at the time, included me
and some Chinese students
I never tired of hearing her
regale them with her short answers
which always led
tension building
into a very large discussion
"Where did you live in China?"
"Tiananmen square"
"Oh, really...when?"
"in 1988 my family moved there
and stayed for 6 years"
"Ah." she would let it sit
before mentioning
that every time
she made her admission
to a Chinese person
they fell silent
"Yes," one breathed
"that's because in China

Softly Glowing Exit Signs

if you talk about the government
or terrible things that have happened
it's like a cane will come from offstage
and grab you away from the audience"

Georgia Park

The Buddha's Lap

I am dyed a rich, complex shade of blue
with purple hues
and gold designs intricately
outlining my stomach and thighs
the sun is baking the colors
into my skin until
the paint starts cracking—
I hear parrots squawking
I am in the jungle
and I'm not afraid of elephants
I keep thinking
one might come near me
and how much
I'd like for it
to be pink
and I would gaze at it
but that doesn't happen
I head for the water
there are bugs all around me
buzzing and I dip my toe into
a stagnant river
the blue spreads like watercolor
I see a statue of Siddhartha
it's stone and the size
of my father
and there is moss
creeping up the side of him

Softly Glowing Exit Signs

his eyes are lowered
into his lap
and I want to crawl
into it so I wade over
to him, grabbing lily pads
as I go, for balance
in the hot, hot sun
most of my color is gone
into the river
which is even more
beautiful now
dyed vibrantly behind me
I splash and dive under
to cleanse myself of it
but as I climb into
the warm stone
I leave a handprint here
there, a vague hint
of a footprint
I cover my mouth
to hide my smiling
and let my feet
dangle over the edge
of his knee
I hold his chest
with my staining hands
I am so warm
in the Buddha's lap
and there is buzzing

Georgia Park

in my ears
moths and dragonflies
are settling
here and there
my cheek warms
on his stomach
and like a statue
I think of nothing

Skyline Again

I totaled my car
directly after seeing you
although it was not a direct result
I understand that this is not your fault.
in fact, the guard rail did it

I couldn't think of anything better
than to come back here
I was flooded by the fact
that I can't remember anything
at all but the ocean

and then
the screeching tires
the screaming
the quiet that follows

I could never see you clearly
I forgot how to talk
and how to listen
I am the person
who totaled my car
I could hear some humming
I think
I bet you remembered
it differently
or at least better than

Georgia Park

not at all
and then, the screaming
the alone, the gulls,
the delay the halting
apologies
the overseas
the wrongs

Are You Gonna Eat That?

Hitting the road again
for the first time since
I smashed my little Korean safety box
across three lanes
the stars, the ocean
and the goddamned highway
the soup
before it spilled on my shirt
with a splattering burn to the chest
hung in the air
for a moment
I thought about nothing
then we hit
I looked over and remembered when
I thought you were something
then all the sudden
you looked like spaghetti strands
were leaking out of your stomach

I Just Got Back

I just got back into the U.S. and someone said
are you sure you want to go back there?
it's getting kind of dangerous
this was an American

I once crossed a border
on my hands and knees in the dirt
to get back to America
where you can drink the water
and there are hospitals
and people speak my language
easily, free flowing
even when my words tumble and fail me
when I'm dehydrating rapidly

where no one mistakes me for a Russian
with all the implications
of being a Russian immigrant woman
alone at night or in the morning

where at least I could call the police
although I wouldn't recommend it
for my baby brother
I've trained him in the art
of not getting shot
for his skin color

Korea had signs up in the bars of Seoul
saying no Africans allowed here

Softly Glowing Exit Signs

because of Ebola
the Thai would not allow their own people in
to the more expensive places
I was run down with a car in Costa Rica
by people sneering *gringa*
I was chased in Panama
and almost kidnapped
on two separate occasions
in Nicaragua the white man pedophilia
was rampant—so they thought
I was with a sex tourist
I dropped out of my own
high school
because they spit at me
and called me gay
I carry mace in the United States
when people come near me
I back away
to where
my aging father is weeping suddenly
and telling all of his children
to run run to Canada
but I just got back here
to be with him
and I'm not leaving
ever again
at least this is a place
I understand

Dangerous Adventures

I'm always careful
to let people know
where I'm going
I leave a paper trail
of hearts and kisses
on a GPS–please track me
and call the police
if I don't make it back
but I don't want to
always live like that

RUN!

Walk of Shame

Once there was a girl
(or boy, it doesn't really matter)
who didn't have a name
(or had one that was shattered)
who wrote too much
then spoke too much
then matured backwards
he or she would only
shut up inside a tavern
and was only seen outside of it
tightroping the distance
between that person's self
and other people's houses

Everybody Talks

Yes, I am a woman
who says she hates men
right before she leaves the bar
with the very worst of them
and people can say
ah, that explains it
I would hate men too
if I put up with that shit
people can say
most anything
while they're still at the bar
sitting there drinking
but at least I'm out there
trying again
at least I'm alive
my heart is pumping

It's Just Another Fun Summer

I am ashamed to admit
that after just three nights of not drinking
I'll have to start the count again

but he followed me into my bedroom
which is, after all, also my kitchen
then he chased me to the liquor store
and while running, I thought
I've never had this much fun before
so, what the hell, why not?

Another Psychiatrist

So it's another appointment
and another brand-new psychiatrist's assessment
in which I'll be re-diagnosed in under twenty minutes
she says I'm too young to be on heart medication
but my problem is a hyperactive amygdala
putting stress on my organs
and causing my heart to beat like a rabbit's
she prescribes yoga and deep breathing
and I say you know it's funny
I used to work out every day
but lately I find I spend most of my time
lying in bed. She says, ah, so you're depressed
and the fact that she didn't phrase it as a question
makes me so incredibly sad

Our Ghost Children

I miss you the most while confiding
in a man who will never understand
the way we used to have tea and whiskey
on your bare, wooden table
while our ghost children played beneath it
mine being several years the senior
having been unborn
when I was barely a teenager
yours I remember
would've been a toddler
since I was the godparent
of your abortion--I like to think
that they are friends. he asks
why I would want to think
of such morbid things
especially since then
in succession, the scene
rushes back so fast

the blood pulsing down
the drain—me doubled over
looking for a fetus in it
because they gave me Demerol
with no instructions on what to expect
and proceeded with such little consent
that I really didn't understand
the doctor who asked

Georgia Park

if I wanted to know the sex
and my fogged-up answer, through tears
no...please...wait...yes
you and I both curled up separately
in different years for days each

he asks if I could try again
and I miss the fact that
you and I both intrinsically
know that I just can't
and you in particular know
never to ask a question like that

Softly Glowing Exit Signs

The Pros and Cons of Being This Heavily Medicated

Since humans are predators
and the females of the species
double as prey
our brains are hard wired
to scan for faces
I used to see his every day

in the grains of the forest
cut down in pieces, sawed into halves
and sanded to make up our living room table
and in the beer puddles, which to me
looked rainbow, but don't anymore

now that my diet consists
of white, chalky Skittles
and I am marshmallowed
to the teeth, I don't see
the faces like I used to
mostly I just fall asleep

I do remember just one tree
I'd carved some initials into
with a knife I don't feel the need
to carry around anymore
but I can't remember the names
and I don't think they'd come to me again

even without the medication
because it wasn't a face
all I could manage
to create at that time was
a scraggly little heart shape

Friendly Advice

"You do realize the information you've given me
about the last two men you were involved with
makes me want to kill them?
and then, what's worse
are the subsequent consequences
no matter how you justify it
something has to give
and you just told me, it's giving."
"Yeah but, I never want to see
either of them again
it's finished.
So, what's the difference
if it even happened?"
"Lilah, I'm concerned
about your mental well being
it's a facade and I can see
that it's crumbling
you just weren't built
to handle these experiences
your consent, when you're even
awake enough to give, it isn't genuine."

"Ok, so what do you expect me to do?
"I want you to see someone
again, please do.
but this time
make it someone experienced

and not just a figment
of your imagination
or some exaggerated version
of a simple school counselor
Lilah, you need to see
someone about it.
I don't want to see
any more men
take advantage.
Lilah, don't you know
you're a human being
just because you haven't
been treated like one
doesn't mean you deserve this."
"You have to admit
I really do bring out
the worst in men."
"Lilah,
they're taking advantage
haven't you heard that expression?"
I remember he said
take this to relax
and now,
spread your legs....
"Lilah? Lilah?
you need to stop
drinking.

Softly Glowing Exit Signs

I'm going to call
someone to help
Someone, help me!"

Doing Without

He had shelter without electricity, plumbing, or heat
when I decided to move in with him
he brought home a traveling porta-potty
placed it at the base of the stairs
in the hallway and hung a shower curtain
so we could make our messes
the ceilings were wooden, rotten
and high beamed

I got a gym membership
just so I could keep clean
the oil on my hair and skin
was almost enough to cook with
but I couldn't prove that
without a kitchen

and I have gotten drunk
so often and laid so many down
spinning around his hovel
and later, alone in my own apartment
to the same old songs
I think by now
I can sustain the feeling
without the alcohol

I tell him that when I see him

Softly Glowing Exit Signs

like old friends with the immediacy
of two people who still speak
he says "Good. You really should've quit
years ago," and I'm puzzled
because had I done that
I never would've grown
to love him, but I smile

Daffodil

There's a little daffodil
well, there are so many things, really
there are doctors and dentists
and baby teeth still connected
where they shouldn't be
dying post-maturely

these are some of the things
I've heard people say about me:
she's a mental patient, an anomaly
and she's annoying
she cries and cries but refuses medication
she says it'd let her guard down

there are lots of cities with different
things and people in them
I can't imagine why I chose this one
but I was mistaken and now I'm stuck here

but there is also a rocky layer
on the shore of the ocean
it's good for balancing on
during difficult conversations
or trying to redirect neural pathways
through positive thinking
via your therapist's instructions

Softly Glowing Exit Signs

or whatever, it's good for walking
and there's a little daffodil
I can't see it, but I know it's there
its strong, wild and vibrantly yellow
and someday, I'll pluck it from somewhere

Hot Pink Iron Lung

My mother had me fitted into my iron lung during my last overdose on barbiturates. "I had it made and shipped to the back door," she later told me, "after the last time you stopped breathing. Honey, I just felt so helpless. I couldn't go through that again, and I thought we might as well cut out the embarrassment with the doctors while we're at it. Save us all a trip. Thank God, the drugs made you thin enough for me to lift and position you into the thing. You were barely ninety pounds then, bless your scrawny little soul."

Yeah...thank God, I wanted to retort. I didn't say it out loud only because that ability had already been taken by the last overdose. We are told that when we die, our souls leave our bodies. My brain lost connectivity with my mouth that night, but nothing else happened. The truth is, I did die, but even if I could talk, I wouldn't hurt my mother's feelings by divulging that information. She tries so hard to keep me hanging on. I wonder if she knows.

She knows how hard I had tried to die. I had tried in boardinghouses across the city, next to the shoes left outside the doorsteps of Asian families living in a single room, breathing the warm, musky smell of Middle Eastern dishes wafting from the rooms upstairs. I almost died in those hallways. I tried again in the various studio apartments and fire escapes of various skinny kids, needles in our veins and powder on our noses. Then I would try walking home alone, with a tank top baring my shoulders to lean against rough brick walls and faltering flip flops introducing the soles of my feet to the hot pavement of the sidewalks and streets. I didn't care if it was a high or a low. I tried. Nothing really hurt back then, aside from the occasional withdrawal.

Trying to fit my key in the door of my mother's house at the end of the journey back was always the hardest part. Which key was it, and was the trick of fitting it in at the right angle or was something wrong with the size or shape of the thing? More importantly, when was it appropriate to give up? Exercising my fine motor skills usually exhausted me to the point of slipping down to the pale pink welcome mat to our front door and having a rest there.

"Geraldine, GERALDINE, wake up!" My mother would scream when she came home to discover me slumped against our door. She'd slap me across the face several times before inevitably dragging me into the living room to have a longer chat in my general direction. At which point I'd tune in and out, always propped up against a pastel colored wall like one of my mother's rag dolls.

Eventually my mother cupped her hand under my chin and lifted my brown eyes to look into the twins of hers. "We need to talk about why you're trying to kill yourself, ok?"

I never got the opportunity to tell her before she sacrificed my voice in order to 'save me from myself'. Not that I ever would have.

To mother's credit, though, she did try to make the confinement fun. She nicknamed my metal casket "Lungy" and painted it hot pink. She would bring home stickers from various skate stores and coffee shops around San Antonio and let me choose where to place them. She even had air conditioning installed on the inside of it, like they do with the animal suits at Disney World.

I knew she had reason to like Lungy. Not only did Lungy help me breathe, but it also kept my hands clean of drugs. I guess it's unsurprising that I was finally able to keep them clean once they were physically contained, constantly bound to my sides.

At first, it was just me, mother and Lungy. I was twenty. I say at first, because that's when I believe my life began. Certainly, it's when I began to see the world, or at least our lavender colored living room with it's the phony flowers and the throw pillows, through clear eyes. It looked like the inside of an Easter egg. The main reason mother had switched me to that room was so that she could have a more or less constant view of me, and I could have a view onto the front yard. She thought I would grow to appreciate that. She would occasionally sit on the loveseat behind me and point things out; my old tire swing measuring the intensity of that day's wind, the neighbors that walked by but never looked in, the occasional jackrabbit.

Mostly, though, I just watched mother. She would wander through the room to dust her little horse figurines and refluff the couch pillows throughout the day, talking on the phone more often than not.

I knew those horse figurines well. Over the past year, I had given each of them a name and had them develop relationships and rivalries with each other. Henry was having an affair with Henrietta the Hermaphrodite from down the row. Of course, because of Henry's strict protestant upbringing, prudish wife and young children, I never witnessed one of his rendezvous with Henrietta, but I saw the way their eyes locked. In addition to the private lives of her horse figurines, my mother's own private life seemed fascinating to me. I lived to see her walk through the living room, and even better, to hear her on the phone, "He said *what*? Well, no wonder she's divorcing him! I would've too!" "No, not Mary with the daughter at Dartmouth, Mary who keeps trying to kill herself. You know, the one with the body odor who works at J. Jill? Good lord, is she ugly! Bless her soul, the last two attempts didn't work."

So often, by her middle-aged years, so many things seemed to turn out to be such a shame. Luckily for her, mother thrived on getting inside knowledge of other people's shame. Brain tumors, financial failures, car crashes, separations and delinquencies, juvenile or otherwise, my mother was the first to know. She really kept in touch with the community.

Nothing perked her up like the announcement of terrible news. "Oh yeah?" I'd hear her gush on the phone, "You mean Jerry, the crackhead? No! Did she report him to the police? Was anyone hurt? No! You don't mean to tell me-" by the time she finished a phone call like that, she'd be humming show tunes and Christmas carols all throughout the house. I guess it made our plight look more manageable to her by comparison. It seemed to

Softly Glowing Exit Signs

take her mind off minor things like our plush rose rug being overdue for a cleaning, or her own dwindling interest in her dead and hopefully convalescing daughter.

Funny, then, that she kept me such a secret. Shrank from the community in the last year with vague excuses that she wasn't feeling well, had better stay in tonight. Or maybe because she didn't want other people to take joy in her scandal, knowing firsthand how vicious that joy can be. How satisfying.

In the mornings, especially after a phone call bearing no horrible news at all, I had her full attention. That was our hair and makeup time. She'd roll Lungy right outside the bathroom and use the extendable shower head to wash my lank, dark brown hair over a bucket. I had thin hair compared to her blond, streaked bouffant, just as I was pale and thin to her plump and rosy cheeked. My eyebrows were thicker than hers, but her thighs were thicker and her breasts were bigger than mine. Other than that, we looked the same. Same pointed nose, same pouty mouth.

She made an effort to add some volume to my hair, always careful to be sure the temperature was to my liking, testing the water on her fingers before my scalp. She continued to tweak the temperature even then, until I smiled and closed my eyes. I liked the water much hotter than she would venture was comfortable. She always started me off with lukewarm water, thinking, I supposed, that someday I might still change my preference to anything less than scalding hot.

Mother was a beauty school dropout who still liked to play dress up and talk about her glory days while washing my hair. "I would never have dropped out of that school if it weren't for your father." She'd sigh. "Oh, of course, money's nice, Geraldine. But I had friends at that school. If there's one thing money can't buy, its friendship. At least with love you can get a prostitute! Go on a dating site! But hang on tight to your friends." I raised my eyebrow. *What friends?* I thought. I turned my head to look up at her, with a carefully constructed expression of consternation. *What friends?* I insisted.

She faltered. Frowned and looked away. "Oh honey, we haven't had much company to the house this past year, have we? I just don't know what people would say. You know, iron lungs went out of style years ago."

I felt an expression of sadness overcome me. Wash. Rinse. Repeat. My mother's hands never stopped lathering, even during one of those times, like now, when her voice shook. I looked into her eyes searchingly until I found guilt. Then I looked away. Closed my eyes.

"Oh, I know! How about a nurse?" I cast a glance upwards and she rewarded it with her face lit up like a Christmas tree. I smiled. She bore me relatively young, and now she was barely forty. She still had great ideas and velour track suits to match her ambitions. She had an exercise machine she called a "stepper" and now, I could tell by her expression, she had research to do and phone calls to make.

"Really, all you need is your feeding tube refilled, catheter emptied and...Well, maybe if there were days I wasn't here...you know, maybe if I wanted to go out, or even...take a weekend away..." She was faltering. I suddenly understood that she had been feeling held back. She still considered herself to be in her prime, and, aside from me, she was single. Maybe she felt tethered to this pastel house by a young, pale daughter in her metallically pink and utterly unspeakable casket. Who's to say the patterns she really wanted to see weren't all flannel, work boot and jean-clad? I felt my face grow hot.

"Honey, I love doing your make-up and spending time with you. Every morning I'm here. But, well, I have friends I go out and see. Or I used to. You should have friends that come in to see you. A companion, people do that. Maybe a beautician, like me. Or like I would've been. And a nurse. Then, baby, if I wanted to go away for the weekend. Well, I'd bring you back something real nice every time. A souvenir!" She eyed her horse figurines. "We can start you up some sort of collection. Maybe castles, or little angels?" I wrinkled my nose.

"Ok, you don't like that." She wrung out my hair and wrapped it in the oversized, fluffy towel she'd kept waiting around her shoulders. "But what about the nurse idea? A companion? Someone to do your hair and makeup and talk to you if I go away for the weekend?" Her tone was hopeful. I had been looking back at the living room window at the old oak tree. It had always been in our front yard, even before the first day of my life, the day I conjoined with Lungy.

I wasn't sure I liked change. But I had come to love my mother very much. I smiled at her.

What followed my mother's idea was a different type of phone call. "Gloria! I haven't talked to you in ages. Don't you think it's about time we caught up? Call me!" It wasn't the phone call that was different, exactly, my mother was nothing if not a social butterfly. But her voice was false, and I recognized the name Gloria. I shot my mother a puzzled look when she finally walked by me in the living room.

"Geraldine, I'm going to make you a friend! I can't believe I ate shit and called Gloria, but she's the only friend I really had in beauty school, and I know she knows people. We also don't have to worry about her blabbing, with the amount of dirt I have on her, she better just watch herself as is!" I raised my eyebrows.

"Oh, I shouldn't tell you. I promised her I'd never tell a soul, and we don't want to bring bad juju around right before she starts keeping our secret for us. On the other hand...who are you going to tell, am I right?"

My mother sat to the pink loveseat parallel to Lungy and braided my hair away from my ear. Then she whispered Gloria's secret into it. Apparently, her son had been molested by one of her boyfriends when he was young, and it was all Gloria could do to keep him out of trouble as an adult. But the real horror of the whole thing was, Gloria never called the police or did anything to stop it. She didn't want to give up the guy. She kept him around until he left her for another woman with small children, at which point she sobbed to my mother over tea, deep, gasping sobs, and admitted everything she had sacrificed for the son of a bitch. She begged my mother not to tell anyone, of course. And technically, my mother never had.

But while I was listening to my mother's scandalous gossip, all I could think about was the fact that she was right, I could never tell anyone the secret, anyways. So, if she had technically kept her promise not to tell anyone, did that make me not anyone to her? The question kept me up all that night.

The phone rang the next day around three. We didn't have a clock in the living room, but I understood by then that when the sun was visible next to the uppermost windowpane, it was early afternoon.

"Hello? ...Gloria, so nice to hear back..." My mother wandered around the house, sometimes stopping with one hand on her hip, staring out the window. Sometimes folding both hands in front of her chest, and sometimes disappearing to a part of the house where I couldn't see or hear her. "Well, the thing is, honestly, I'd prefer a beautician to a nurse. Anyone can be taught to change a catheter, but those nurses take themselves so seriously. Plus, aren't they mandated reporters? Right. Not like I'm doing anything wrong, but...exactly. Oh Gloria, I knew you'd understand. Do you know anyone?"

I woke to my mother laying on the plastic covered purple loveseat parallel to Lungy and I, stroking what felt like circle designs into my cheek.

"Geraldine," She whispered, and I opened my eyes to blink at the ceiling. "Good morning, sweetie. Guess what?" I looked at her, and she smiled. "We're having company today!"

My mother hadn't done her own hair and make-up yet. She must have woken up in the middle of the night to come sleep next to me. She looked so drawn without her makeup, her lips pale as the circles under her eyes were dark, her plump cheeks not looking rosy at all, but white as my own. I caught sight of a couple spare greys in her unkempt bouffant. She looked as drained as I used to feel when I sank down to the floor. I wanted to reach out and stroke her cheek back, but of course, I couldn't.

"I think I finally know how you used to feel when you would run away, sweetie. I feel like I'm drowning here sometimes with you." Here, she avoided my eyes. "I remember when we first got Lungy. Honey, your catheter would overfill and I would leave you there, avoiding opening Lungy for as long as I could. I knew you were wet, and then I knew your pants must've dried after a certain amount of time, and that made me feel better. But I have to admit, I haven't taken very good care of you at all." I took my eyes off hers and turned in the other direction. I remembered the smell of urine, the wet in my pants that turned cold after only a few minutes, the itch as it dried, the discomfort. The footsteps trying to move as quietly as possible in and out of the front door, avoiding me.

I wanted to tell her that she'd gotten better. I looked back at her, painful as it was, and smiled. After all, she was all I had now. I sensed her slipping away from me again, and that was the last thing I wanted.

"Everything will be different now. Gloria's sending her own son to come take care of you. You were so little, I don't know if you'll remember, but you two played together when you were toddlers. Remember Robby Jr?" Robby Jr? I thought, one of the beautician's sons...the one who'd been molested? I remembered playing Barbie dolls with a little towheaded boy. I remembered wondering where his sister was and if she'd be angry he was playing with all of her Barbie dolls. Then I remembered him ripping the head off of one of them and using it as a ping pong ball.

"He's all grown up now, anyways, and following in Gloria's footsteps, a beautician. Probably gay, although Gloria would never admit it if he was. I don't want to interview anyone we don't know personally for the role of your caretaker, so I'm really hoping this goes well, sweetheart. Will you do me a favor and smile at him? I know you haven't given me much trouble in the last couple of years, but you were such a handful before Lungy. Promise me you'll behave?"

I was becoming nervous. My mother had never talked about her neglect of me in Lungy before, never made these confessions, never told anyone about me as far as I knew. We certainly hadn't had any outside visitors since I had been conjoined with Lungy. I turned my head away only to hear her sigh and the plastic of the loveseat cover crinkle as she made her way into the bathroom. She knew me well. For the first time in over a year, I found I didn't *want* to behave. I heard the bathroom door shut and the shower turn on as I gazed out the window. The sun was high in the sky by then, the clock on the cable box reading 9:00 am.

I bet he'd come for dinner, so mother could liquor him up a bit before the introductions. Not that she couldn't do the same at brunch, but if it were brunch she would've been ready hours early and had something in the oven by now. She wouldn't have found the time to softly etch circles into my cheek with her manicured nails or make undue confessions.

There wasn't a lot of traffic on our street. It must have been a windy day outside, because my old tire swing was swinging back and forth from the elm tree as steadily as a pendulum. I preferred to count the tiny holes in our ceiling tiles rather than watch the sun slowly change position in the sky or watch the tire swing moving with the wind instead of with me. The last time I used the swing it was to avoid going inside at the end of the school day. I might have been ten, but already starting my teenage angst. I'd listen to the alternative rock station on my Walkman and twist around, letting the rope untwist me over and over. My mother was usually out until nightfall anyways in those days. After work, she liked to go out drinking. My dad was gone by then.

Softly Glowing Exit Signs

I fall asleep on the two hundred and thirty-third hole in our ceiling, before I even hear the shower turn off.

By the time I wake up, there is the smell of a roast coming from the oven, and my mother is prancing around in the living room with her silver heels on. Her perfume is so strong it might have been just the thing that woke me up, even from clear across the room, where she is dusting Henrietta's father, Richie.

I wonder if Richie knows about Henrietta's affair, and if so, how he feels about it. Would he reveal it to Henrietta's mother, or try to protect her from the truth, seeing as how she was missing a leg, and already placed behind the rest of the family to hide her own disfigurement? Even though Henrietta's parents supported her throughout her gender identity crisis, I feel sorry for both families involved in the extramarital love affair. A lot of horse figurines are going to be hurt when the truth comes out, I think. My mother is humming a Christmas song nervously, warping the intended tune into what sounds like electronica.

I'm so absorbed in the horse figurines, as I usually am before falling asleep and right after waking up, that it takes me a minute to gather from my mother's dress and nervous energy that it must be go time. She's in her maroon dress, with the Spanx on, from the looks of it. She's also wearing her pearls with the jade elephant medallion, always a conversation piece, just a little aside from the traditional simple strand. That probably means she was afraid there wouldn't be much to talk about and has been rehearsing anecdotes from her long-ago trip to China as a plan B.

Then, predictable as clockwork, my mother spots me awake, "Geraldine, have I ever told you about my trip abroad to China when I was in high school? Oh, it was awful," she says, as if to herself, turning back to her figurines. "All that smog, and those poor people. You could just feel the oppression in the air. I'll tell you; I've never been so happy to be in the good old U S of A as I was after coming home from that trip! Never left home again, in fact! But when I saw that poor little beggar girl selling jewelry, well, my heart went out to her, and the next moment, there I was with this necklace! It's just a coincidence that it happens to be beautiful enough to still wear! Real pearls? Oh, no, dear. My good pearls are upstairs. I have to say; I prefer these sometimes! Sentimental value, you know."

Mother jumps when she hears the knock at the door. It sounds like the police. She shoots me a faltering smile. "Oh, that must be Robby, now." She ventures off of the plush rug and out of my eyesight, her heels clicking over the tile hallway leading up to our front door to receive him. "Robby! Is that you?"

"Sure is, Mrs. Carella."

"Oh, of course it is! How wonderful. Come in, come in."

I hear clicking heels backwards into the hall, joined by what sounds like a gentleman's tap shoes.

"Should I take my shoes off?" His voice is not one I recognize, not the screech and whine of little Robby Jr. It's a deep and penetrative sound, like bees buzzing. Or flies. My mother's is of a higher pitch than normal. More desperate sounding.

"Oh no, dear, I didn't wear these heels just to leave them at the door. The shoes pull together the whole outfit."

"I agree. You look great."

"Thank you. And you, well, you've certainly grown up, haven't you? Here, come into the kitchen, have a seat. Would you like a drink? A cola, maybe, or some bourbon? Wine? Whiskey? Ginger ale? Coffee, tea? I've got a little milk, here, enough to fill a glass."

"I wouldn't mind some bourbon."

"Smart man! I'll make one on rocks for each of us."

In the space occupied by the sounds of clinking ice and more than the usual amount of liquid pouring, Robby misses his opportunity to compliment my mother on her lovely home. *Strike one*, I think, smugly satisfied. I want him to fail, to be kicked out of our family of two as soon as possible. The more he doesn't know the rules, misses the cues prompting these desired responses: "What a lovely home," "What a lovely dress," "Mothers are Gods' angels sent right down from heaven," the further I can feel from his bee swarm voice, his Barbie head pulling antics, his possible molestation. The safer I can feel, warm in my cocoon.

My wishes are interrupted by the noise of my mother setting Robby's glass in front of him and pulling out a chair for herself to sit on. "So, Robby, your mother tells me she's set up a wonderful duplex for you on Sycamore Street?"

"Yeah, it's nice and roomy. She was hoping I would find someone to share my part, but honestly, I think I'm better off alone. I have enough company as it is and I really don't like too much mess.

"Oh, I completely agree! I'm a bit of a neat freak myself, but I can't stand cleaning up other people's messes. My Geraldine-I trust your mother has told you? Yes, Geraldine, it's tragic, what happened to her, but I have to say, she is so much cleaner now. No crumbs, no roaming around at night, no attitude. Of course, for a mother, it can be hard to be left with so much...nothing. Nothing where there used to be so much something is sad, you know. Even if it's replacing...well, we had some unpleasant times before the accident, but...Anyways, I was just saying, for someone who isn't attached, someone whose not her mother, she's really no trouble to have around. No dishes and no dirt, at least. And she's mute."

"Sounds like a dream roommate."

"Yes! She really would be." Mother sounds relieved while I am feeling more and more unsettled. Unadulterated confessions are not her usual style, and they don't suit her well. "Well, the roast will be ready soon, are you terribly hungry?"

"I am, a little," he admitted.

"Oh, of course you are, poor thing! It's been so long since I had a young man in the house! Lee me get some crackers and cheese, the roast will be ready in just about...ah! Here, it looks about done now." The sound of mother creaking open the oven door followed by the scent of a slightly burnt roast wafts in to my nose from the kitchen. She chatters on, nervously, and it sounds like she was setting the table. I wonder what I would enjoy more after over a year without each, the booze or the food. I wonder which would make me more sick after using a feeding tube for as long as I had. My mother chatters on and on.

"You're a little early. Not that I'm complaining, I was on pins and needles to see you again, I haven't seen you since you were...you must have been about six. Do you remember coming here and playing with Geraldine?"

"I don't. But I have to admit, I really don't remember much before the age of twelve."

"Well, I guess I don't remember too much from my childhood at this point, either. Geraldine became sort of surly when she hit her early teens and said the same thing. But you must at least remember me? Your mother and I were thick as thieves while we were at beauty school, split our childcare right down the middle between us. You were always either at her house with Geraldine or mine. You used to call me Auntie Glo, do you remember? I just loved that name!"

"I'm sorry, I don't remember."

There is an uncomfortable silence. "Ah, well," My mother amends. "We had fun. Your mother and I used to let you and Geraldine make us up. We have pictures, somewhere-you'd put lipstick all over your mother's chin. But I hear you've continued as a beautician?"

"Yeah, I'm mostly self-taught, off of YouTube."

"And those tattoos, are they drawn on?"

"No, these tattoos are real. I designed them myself."

"Ah. Charming. What does that one on your neck mean? I can't quite make it out."

"Oh, nothing in particular. It's all just art to me. Part of the aesthetics, the beautification process. I would love to practice on Geraldine."

"Oh, yes! She is a perfect mannequin! Such a beautiful face. Of course, not nearly as beautiful as mine, but..." I imagine my mother was gesturing toward her face and fluttering her eyelashes, an over exaggerated and overused joke that apparently goes unappreciated by Robby Jr. I start to take an interest in Robby. Tattoos on his neck? Why isn't my mother more put off by that? He doesn't seem to have much personality, yet my mother is striving to charm him. I guess she just really wants those few nights on the town away from me. I want to meet this Robby and compare him the cruel, towheaded boy of my early memories. Maybe he's changed.

"I could even take her home with me tonight. I know the agreement; I have my van here with me. I brought the ramp."

"Oh! That's so wonderful! Of course, you'll have to meet her. Have you had enough to eat, dear? Can I take your plate?"

An assenting grunt, the sound of tables being cleared and my heart fluttering in my chest. They'll be coming to appraise me in just a moment. He's taking me away tonight. In a *van*. My mother had called a man with neck tattoos and pre-arranged for him to have a van to take me into the night. All for a pre-arranged fee, I'm sure, a large lump sum, and then she fed him roast. She hasn't fed me a roast in years. My heart starts pounding in my ears more violently. I squeeze my eyes shut. I will not open them again until I am being loaded into the van.

I will not reward my mother with a look she could interpret as a nod of assent or a terrified protest. I will not lay eyes on her again. I also no longer want to reveal the monster of Robby Jr. to myself. I will ignore the whole appraisal.

I ignore the wheels of Lungy struggling over the shag carpet then gliding easily over the tiled floor of the front hallway. I ignore my neck rising and falling against Lungy as I am jostled out the front door. It's harder to ignore the smell of the plants, the suburban lawn, the night air hitting my pallid face. The first stair, the second, the third, will they lose control of Lungy? No. They should've called for more help; I shouldn't be jostled this much. I feel sick. My wheels on gravel. My wheels on a ramp. A door slamming.

I'm not secured inside the van. I am a thing on wheels inside of a thing on wheels. What kind of an idiot is this idiot? My mother didn't say anything about loading me into a van and not securing me?

As the van starts moving, so does Lungy, of course. My head bashes into the front of the storage unit every time Robby Jr. slows or comes to a halt. Once or twice, I'm sure the top of my head hits so hard it leaves bruises. I also assume he can hear the crashing from the storage unit, which has to be directly behind his seat. In any case, he does nothing about it. I fall into long, blank sleeps and wake up thirsty several times over. There are no windows in the back. It's dark the whole time.

I don't know how much more time passes before the van eventually stops. I hear the driver's side of the car open and Robby Jr. coming around the side to open the back door.

"Here we are, dolly, steady as she goes!" His voice sounds a lot more unhinged than it was during the polite dinner conversation with my mother. I want to tell him I'm going anywhere with him, that I need to be with my mother. When I remember that my mother and I seem to hold differing opinions on this subject, I want him to like me better than my mother. I want him to let me into a secret world, do my hair, and talk to me every day. I don't know if I mind being someone's dolly. Then the moment passes, and I am frightened again.

He is a hulking figure with apparent strength behind his dawdling words. He wheels me down a ramp and up one. I guess his place was already wheelchair accessible. Well, of course, what did I expect, a cannon to shoot me in? I can't see much in the dark and I have no idea how far into the building we've gone. I didn't hear a door shut behind us and I can still smell the outside air. Are there palm trees now surrounding us, cacti? Are we outside or in? Have I lost my sight?
The air smells sweet and I hear cicadas for the first time in over a year. Then again, I haven't been outside in that long.

"You haven't been *alive* in that long." Robby murmurs as he pushes me along.

Wait a minute, is he listening in on my thoughts? I didn't say that out loud.

"No, you didn't think you could speak at all, did you?" he asks, and I crane my neck to catch an impossible twinkle in his hardened eye. That shuts me up. This can't be real. A false death and an iron lung I can stomach, but being heard again makes all the time I spent imprisoned in my own mouth seem like a waste.

"A false death?" He asks, "You're not so much like your mother. I know you don't have the inclination to fool yourself like she does."

"I'm dead." I say. It's a statement. He doesn't say anything. "Where are you taking me?" I ask.

"Would you really like to know?" I can't answer that. "I'd like to get you out of your casket, first of all," he offers.

"I'll be crippled after being bedbound so long."

"And yet, your voice sounds fine after half an eternity of not speaking."

"Has it been that long?"

"No, only a year, to get your mother over the grieving process. Would you like to walk again?" He asks.

"What's next?"

"You'll have to wait and find out,"

"Will it be worse than life on Earth was for me?" He doesn't say anything, and I don't either. The cicadas are now screaming in my ears. I can't decide whether I like the sound or hate it.

"I'll wait," he told me.

SOFTLY GLOWING EXIT SIGNS

Décor and Decorum

Like a monk
walking barefoot at dawn
to collect his alms
I collect notes of recommendation
based on small acts of kindness
and a bald-faced willingness to lie
transcripts, bills I can't begin to pay
and anticipate rejection slips
from several publications
I wait by the mailbox to intercept these
before my roommates see them

So, not like a monk, exactly
sorry

but every one of them is piling up
I will be typecast in lettering
by my brand-new season
they will say "there she goes
a poet! and an American
just like the rest of us
warmongering bastards"

like a monk collecting alms
in Thailand
I have become décor and decorum
to the scenery of my homeland

Georgia Park

I amble past the red lights
and through the pirates
that stumble drunkenly upon me
I walk stiltedly on my old streets
instead of all that drifting
drifting out to sea

The Cashier and the Woman

The cashier with his oily slicked back hair
is stern with the woman
who is looking at her purchases
and seems to really need
those cigarettes

he berates her
with those gimpy legs
—surely she's walked there—
saying every day you bring me change
every day!

and I need dollars
she clutches her quarters and looks puzzled
she says money is money
and then loses her language

her margarine colored hair
pasted with sweat to her forehead
her skin sagging further
according to this predicament
I wonder what he thinks of her
and her blank expression
there is a long silence
before he gives her
just one last chance
and she takes it

Georgia Park

When the Fire Displaced us

I told my displaced neighbors
it was something I did
oh how I knew it
I wasn't as nice
as I could've been
to a dear, old friend
and I skipped out on thanksgiving
they sighed and said, oh
so you're the one who did it

Lost and Found in the Rubble

Raking through the rubble you can find
some embarrassing artifacts like Chin's
the Filipino phlebotomist who liked to collect
no, *hoard*, diamond earrings
and because Chin survived the fire
this leads to awkward questions
"Do you like to wear them?"
"No, god no. My ears aren't pierced
and I don't dress like a woman."
"Were they an inheritance?
Do you have a girlfriend?"
"Look. I don't know, ok
I just like them."

There is also the boy dog
with girl clothes at home
that no one has ever seen him
wear in the light of day before
there is the classy, professional woman
who didn't want anyone to know
she chain-smoked the cheapest cigarettes
there is also this overheard question:
"How much eggnog were you planning to drink?"
and then there are the less surprising things

the immigrants' passports
which remain missing

Georgia Park

smoldered out probably
and buried beneath the ceiling
which is now pasted to the floor
the tenant who had lost his mother
and now, her urn

The Smell of Disaster

Life goes on for them
like it does for me after a stranger's death
I can't look at the news or the social media updates
of my friends. Time is still for me like this cold,
unmoving fog
I am stuck in. So, I tried still going to work after it
happened
because I thought that would make sense
and I fell asleep during a meeting in front of
everyone
I excused myself to get an energy drink from the
vending machine
which I never drink. It worked for fifteen minutes,
then I had to get another
and I felt so sick. Life goes on, except it is more and
more
embarrassing. I don't think I got a chance to comb
my hair
and my clothes smelled like disaster that first day
only now do I realize it was charity to even let me
come in

Georgia Park

How to Keep Working Through a Crisis

On top of all the phone calls you have to make
the emails you have to write, the appointments
you have to schedule and keep, the hygiene and
remembering to eat
it is vital to remember the three most important
things:
phone, wallet, and keys

Spiraling Questions

What if I recklessly wrote three or four poems a day
and sent them into the void of cyberspace
where anyone from my little brother
to my exes could read them
until I was picked clean like the carcass
of the rotisserie chicken my aunt
sent me home with last weekend
and I boiled a bone broth with me in it
could you see my malnourishment
all water with shiny oil spills fed to the masses
at the homeless shelter I almost wound up at

or should I instead demand a little privacy
when the car of my body stops short and my brain
reels back and jolts violently against my skull
until I am irrevocably damaged? should I put on display
for the purpose of a social science I don't understand
the spots where I am worn thin or damaged?
or should I grow out my hair to its natural color
and pile it on top of my head, don sweatpants, do yoga
think about the best exercises for an aging woman
go to therapy, read thick novels, think of children
and bake my very first contribution to Thanksgiving?

Just a pumpkin pie, nothing fancy. Could I possibly forget what happened to me (was it me, really, even back then?)
or at least stop talking about it and just go quiet could mine pass for a brain that's not short circuiting?

Community

How many hours have I spent waiting in line for food stamps
long enough to get familiar with the grooves on the woodblock
attached to the bathroom key I massaged
while navigating my way through some of the future students
I ended up teaching, who later let themselves into my new apartment
as a class to put together my bed frame and deep clean the kitchen
after my last apartment caught fire while I was in it

Fire and Rebirth

The fire is stunning
not to be ignored
from red to yellow to blue
licking everything
I used to love

I wonder if that tree
was dead before
the lightning cleaved
its branches
now scattered
at its own roots
as if bowing down
for the fire to consume

and if so, for how long?
was it dead when I carved
my lover's initials on?
and what could be more beautiful
and more horrifying
than this glittering deconstruction
of the ancient arrangements
which shaded my daily footpath
ever since I started walking?

maybe the modest beginnings
of the next year's saplings

Softly Glowing Exit Signs

this new exposure to the sun
the view's expansion

Turning Tricks

My studio apartment
is not exotic--it's hopelessly American
my life isn't glamourous but in it
to him, a simple American
I am an object of fascination
I perform my tricks
he says, *that's gross*
then admits, *it's also kind of sexy*
before he can decide how he feels about it
I pull him in for a kiss

Put the Newspaper Down First
This is Bound to Make a Mess

The next time I have sex
(I'll invite someone from my contacts list
doesn't much matter which)
I will light candles
and spread newspaper
on my floor
murmuring threats like
I'm going to devour you whole
I will have paints
we can dip our hands into
then touch each other all over
as evidence that I've let this happen
our touches will leave
the prettiest of colors
just as soon as I can afford
to surrender myself again

Bits of Butterfly

I kiss you because I see
softly glowing exit signs
in your eyes and
bits of butterfly
dripping down the
sides of your mouth
I want to catch them
before they fall down
into your shirt
which I take off
just to make sure
to catch the warmth
fluttering from your
chest, I press mine
against it
I don't know
what kind of bugs
are down further
but I want to find out
so I take off your pants
I let you come closer
I curl up inside you
as my cocoon
and I don't come out
until I am cured

Mornings

Plunge the bread into the eggs
pull it out dripping
toss it in the frying pan
bacon and coffee
oil leap frogging
burning skin
and then
your hand
over my hand

Vacation Over

Since I was prescribed medication
which made me stop dreaming
I never thought I'd see him again
and when I did we were both on vacation
he with his wife and child, I with my boyfriend
he drifted so close that I recognized him
by the scent of Dial soap and Marlboros
when I turned my head I could've measured his beard
I almost slipped past until he held me with his eyes
and asked "Aren't you glad to see me again?"
my hands fumbled until they found a railing behind me
so I could hide my knees buckling and stare back thinking
every man I've dated up until recently has looked like him
finally, I said "Excuse me," and I sidestepped

This House

The leftover scraps
from our breakfast
bacon, eggs, coffee
cream and sausages
the image of my feet
wrapped around your legs
dancing in my head
and languishing on the counter
while I'm washing the dishes
this house feels empty without you in it

Fractions

I dreamt I was teaching a group of young women
how to survive trauma inflicted by men
on the first day, I wrote on the board
"You don't owe him anything"
and a woman said "Come on
we already knew that
we just need to know
how to be whole again
after it happens,"
and everyone agreed
I said, "I'm sorry then
I'm actually not qualified
to teach this class
I can only deal in fractions"
and in the fog of silence
I adjusted my glasses

The Sixties

I have wanted to live in a small town
since I spent the summer with my father
and he re-introduced me to his best friend, Chris
who, he told me in confidence, used to be handsome
believe it or not, and I didn't, until I mentioned his name
to my mother, who blushed--my father took me to a local concert
and he and Chris laughed after one song had been played
because, they explained, the singer wrote it about a tryst
he had with a woman who has since married and moved on
and they pointed her out. she was dancing
while her husband sat silent. they were all in their sixties
and I decided I wanted to curate my own disjointed histories

Tonight, I found an enemy in common with a woman
who said that she was thirty-two now and didn't care any more
but this guy had cheated on her with our friend Ariel

nine years before and she'd said "honey, if he'll cheat on me
he'll keep on cheating." Ariel didn't listen, but she was right
it happened --then I met that guy ten years later
and he tried to cheat with me on his girlfriend
I imagine someday we'll all be at a local concert
clucking our tongues at whatever romantic situation
he can wrangle up by the time he's sixty
secretly flushed with shame and secretly laughing

Puppy Supplies

A training certificate, a rabies tag and vaccination checklist
my manic torpedo of energy converted into a process known as nesting
a cage I call a "house" for his benefit (although his vocabulary's limited)
a well-loved pig's ear (all that is well-worn becomes progressively disgusting)
anxiety and depression subsiding, my need for psychotropic medications, waning…
a corner for vomiting, a collar, two tags: one for proof of vaccination, one with his name on it
and oh, a name—I knew I forgot something! Plus the endless supply of tiny bags for pooping
two bowls, food, treats, emotional support card and registration with the letter from my therapist
and oh god, look at his dreadlocks, and so, a groomer, and that breath! A toothbrush,
an endless store of patience I didn't know existed
and what I get in return is
a reason for living—I don't want to remember the time before I had these things

Desk Job

(Do you miss me?)

The office door doesn't shudder
when I walk in
no one takes notice
I'm given a signature
an official stamp
and a desk with a drawer
housing baby carrot sticks
and the book I'm secretly reading

my cubicle walls are all encircling
and decorated with pictures of him
hearts and references

I write a report
I do it again
I drive home
I go to sleep
I wake up in the morning
while he is still sleeping
he doesn't know
how much I kiss him

sometimes, he shields his face
sometimes, he doesn't

but he never remembers
by midday, when I call him

A Lack of Etiquette
ruined my plans to elope

"I'm so happy for you! As long as I'm invited I don't care what you do!"
Should've been: "I'm so happy for you! As long as you're happy too."
But my fiancé thinks differently
So now we are looking at a thirty-person wedding

This Won't be the Event of the Year
So You Don't Get to Cry About It

Never has anyone been more pissed
than your narcissistic family
when you announce your wedding plans
instead of asking their permission
my aunt has excommunicated me
because the wedding is in April
and she's out of town that week
I offered to change the month of the reception
but not the year--and she's still fuming
let me be clear: I am only having this wedding
for the benefit of my husband
and his family, who have never
(not once!) excommunicated him
my dress will be simple
the food will be sufficiently sparse
the people who are no longer invited
can keep their goddamn fuss
it won't be a who's who
of who hasn't spoken to each other in years
there won't be passive aggressive comments
about what is too flashy or not flashy enough
there'll just be clean, white linens
and an open bar
for the people who don't get nasty
when they get drunk
and it'll be just two people

Softly Glowing Exit Signs

in the wedding party
being sure and sweet
in their commitment to each other
because that's all that this day
is supposed to mean

On Becoming a Wife

It's just a piece of paper
one I'd be more than willing to burn
if it were a receipt with which
my new husband could return me
I minimize by claiming
it's mainly for insurance and tax purposes
that nothing will change
except I have decided to take his last name
if only to sever myself from my past on the internet
I'll now be sharing half of my apartment
until we can save up for the house he said he wanted
with an extra bedroom or two for my foster children
and my latest hobby is pretending to be a horrible cook
while I am actually tricking him into eating vegetables
I have processed and blended into a sauce
over what he thinks is spaghetti
 but is actually noodle shaped squash

Make More Money

A well-to-do friend sent me a corporate job listing
so I could make more money at the same instant
a student with Down's Syndrome entered my office
dressed like Santa Clause and offered me a candy cane
So it's settled: I love my job and I'm never leaving

The Day's Ending

We were slightly too old to play such a game
ranging in age from twelve to seventeen
my five pale white-headed cousins and I
decided to take a stance against the tide coming in
in a fruitless effort to resist the day's ending
we were spread out like icecaps dotting the sea
except we kicked, grabbed handfuls of foam
threw them at one another and screamed

there were three left at the last funeral
there will be just two by the next wedding
Joseph, who told Serena I was bitten by a shark
when our two eldest cousins carried me away
that day, after I scraped my knee on a rock
succumbed to a heroin addiction
almost ten years ago now
Laura had kids and stopped talking to anyone
it's almost the same as Erik
except he felt the need to change continents
to get away from us, and Matt?
we never quite figured out
what happened to him
except that he's possibly autistic
and last we heard, driving trucks

tomorrow, I will play a game
for which I am slightly too young

Softly Glowing Exit Signs

I will fight the waves of sleep
brought on by my latest medication
and doze through my ending days
unless I kick and throw and scream
it will be as if I am bleeding out
after a shark has bitten me

and maybe, like that day at the sea
right after I was carted off
someone will take Joseph's place
and tell a ridiculous lie about it
until Serena, still the youngest
will break down crying
and be afraid of the tides
forever after the false ending
was whispered into her small ear
but before the malicious lie of the shark bite
from that little boy, Joseph

our parents said something worse
"When the tide comes in
we'll have to go home
because there will be no place
for your sore old parents to sit"
and it brings me joy to remember
how angry we were about the day's ending
each time I drift into sleep again
without meaning to do it

Georgia Park

The Crow's Funeral

Otters hold hands so they don't drift apart from
each other in the water
cows have best friends
elephants and crows hold funerals
one of which I just witnessed
when a truck came speeding down our street
while a crow was lowering
I have not witnessed a mass shooting
or too much violence yet
outside of what I've observed floating above myself
through the art of dissociation
but as I was weeping on the side of the road
calling the police and wildlife management
because this crow unfortunately
did not die upon his contact with the truck
quite as suddenly as I did
the other crows joined in

Hanging On

Vitamins, steam treatments
bananas, organic greens
smoothies, intravenous
medicine, coconut water
any flavor to keep me
drinking but tea
is too much effort
lotions, Vaseline
I am too young
to struggle so expensively
just to hang on
to this little life
I'm living
but I'm not ready yet
to leave it

The End of an Era

I have to own up
to what can happen to me
dissect and theorize
until I understand it

because I have to make sure
it never happens again

What happens when you "go crazy?"
my therapist asks.
It's a blur...I don't know it's...
Like nothing. Let me think about it.

Are you ready to talk about it yet?
What happens when you "go crazy?"
Yes. I stop counting time
or time stops counting to me
I go on long walks
until the sun rises and sets
and my feet blister
I bump into things
so hard it bruises or bleeds
but I don't feel it

in the early days
before I started to try to control it
I would drink or do drugs

Softly Glowing Exit Signs

in recent years, the drinking
has put me in dangerous situations
because when I drink from that position
I drink really hard
until I don't know what's happening
when people pick me up

And what sets it off?

it used to be a lot of things
baby carriages, pregnancies
the way some people would talk to me
movies, TV scenes, certain songs
and worst of all, love
now it's just this boy I used to know
when I was young

and do you have to understand it anymore?
is this an ongoing experiment?
No, it can't be, so no, it's not
Why is that?
Because it could kill me

Very good. I think we're done.

That's All, Folks!

Am I done now? Am I cured?
Do I not even have to write
tortured poetry anymore?
maybe all I have left to say
is I'm sorry to my brother
because I lost his Airpods case

Softly Glowing Exit Signs

Where to?

Each place I left had a special perk
in the backyard or the neighborhood
I thought I could never live without
mountain, beach, dog cafe, dog park
but I kept moving, so I saw it all
one day maybe we will live against
an active volcano like in Omnetepe
who wrote about that, again?
was it Mark Twain?
or a Japanese garden
and a pond filled with koi fish
or a museum filled with squatters
who pay rent by replenishing the artwork
but I think I'd rather whittle away my days
sitting here with you, remembering

www.ingramcontent.com/pod-product-compliance
Lightning Source LLC
Chambersburg PA
CBHW030329100526
44592CB00010B/631